# You'll Always Be
# NUMBER ONE

*Starr Dunbar*

AuthorHouse™
1663 Liberty Drive
Bloomington, IN 47403
www.authorhouse.com
Phone: 833-262-8899

This book is printed on acid-free paper.

ISBN: 978-1-6655-3901-2 (sc)
ISBN: 978-1-6655-3900-5 (e)

Print information available on the last page.

Published by AuthorHouse  09/22/2021

authorHOUSE®

**You'll Always Be Number One**

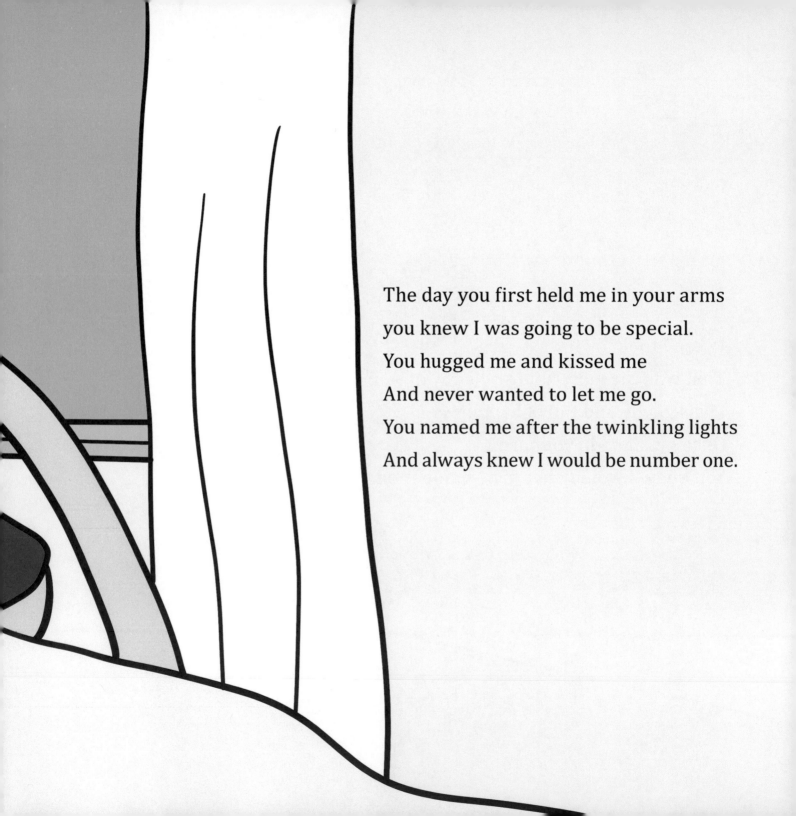

The day you first held me in your arms
you knew I was going to be special.
You hugged me and kissed me
And never wanted to let me go.
You named me after the twinkling lights
And always knew I would be number one.

When I took my first steps

That was the most important day of your life.

I was giggly and full of happiness.

Once I walked in your arms

You knew I would always be number one.

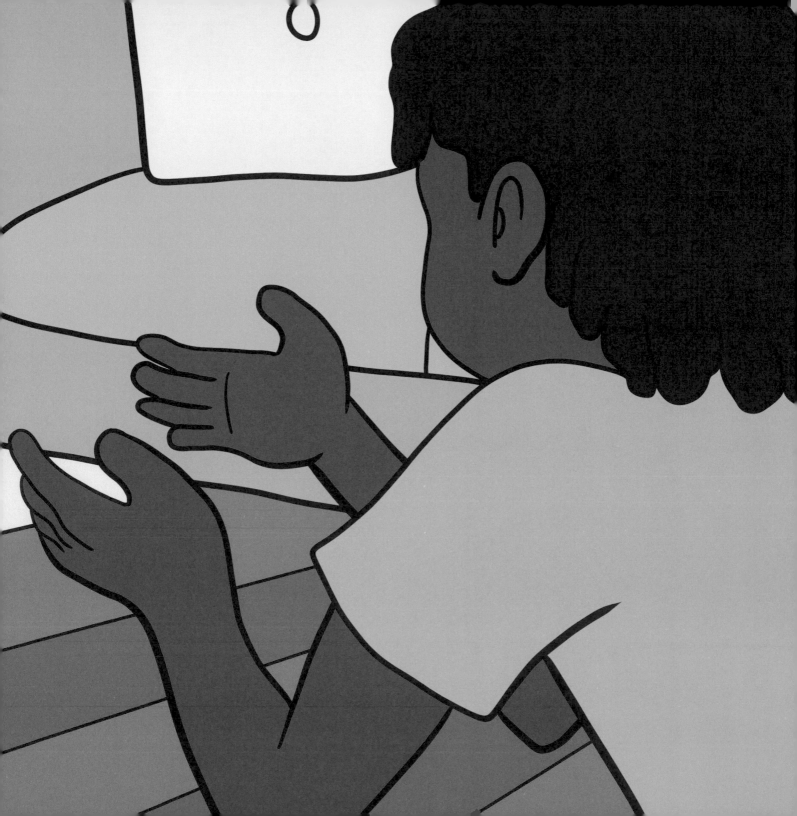

you would read me stories
And tuck me in at night.
I was so calm and precious.
Every night, before you left the room,
you would say "you'll always be what?"
And I answered "number one."

When things weren't going well in your life
You would hide that from me because
You wanted me to see my mama being strong.
You would reassure me that everything is fine
Because I was your number one

At times I made you feel like
the best mom,
I was your light and I was your
Number one.

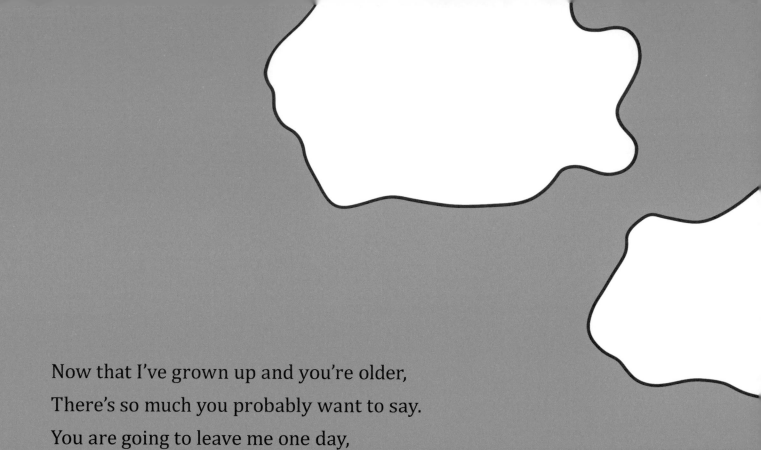

Now that I've grown up and you're older,
There's so much you probably want to say.
You are going to leave me one day,
But I know I will be ok.

I'll be the twinkling light in the sky,

Be giggly and full of happiness,

Always be calm and precious,

Be your light because this won't be

The last I'll hear you say......

**"You'll always be what?"** and I answer **"number one"**.

Printed in the United States
by Baker & Taylor Publisher Services